# First World War
## and Army of Occupation
# War Diary
## France, Belgium and Germany

3 CAVALRY DIVISION
Divisional Troops
7 Light Armoured Battery
1 July 1916 - 29 June 1917

WO95/1146/2

The Naval & Military Press Ltd
www.nmarchive.com
**Published in association with The National Archives**

Published by

## The Naval & Military Press Ltd

Unit 10 Ridgewood Industrial Park,

Uckfield, East Sussex,

TN22 5QE England

Tel: +44 (0) 1825 749494

www.naval-military-press.com

www.nmarchive.com

*This diary has been reprinted in facsimile from the original. Any imperfections are inevitably reproduced and the quality may fall short of modern type and cartographic standards.*

**© Crown Copyright**
**Images reproduced by permission of The National Archives, London, England, 2015.**

# Contents

| Document type | Place/Title | Date From | Date To |
|---|---|---|---|
| Heading | WO95/1146/2 3 Cavalry Division Divisional Troops 7 Light Armoured Battery July 1916-June 1917 | | |
| Heading | 3rd Cavalry Division. WO95/1146 7th Light Armoures Battery. M.M.G.S. July 1916-June 1917. | | |
| War Diary | Corbie | 01/07/1916 | 04/07/1916 |
| War Diary | Hallencourt | 08/07/1916 | 08/07/1916 |
| War Diary | Dadurs | 11/07/1916 | 17/07/1916 |
| War Diary | Bronfay Farm | 25/07/1916 | 26/07/1916 |
| War Diary | Daours | 01/08/1916 | 01/08/1916 |
| War Diary | Gapennes | 04/08/1916 | 04/08/1916 |
| War Diary | Coupelle Neuve | 10/08/1916 | 11/09/1916 |
| War Diary | Neuilly-Le-Dieut | 12/09/1916 | 12/09/1916 |
| War Diary | Belloy-Sur Somme | 14/09/1916 | 14/09/1916 |
| War Diary | Vecquemont | 15/09/1916 | 15/09/1916 |
| War Diary | La Neuville | 17/09/1916 | 17/09/1916 |
| War Diary | Vecquemont | 22/09/1916 | 22/09/1916 |
| War Diary | Crouy | 23/09/1916 | 23/09/1916 |
| War Diary | Villers L'Hopital | 24/09/1916 | 24/09/1916 |
| War Diary | Regnauville | 25/09/1916 | 25/09/1916 |
| War Diary | Wailly Beaucamp | 30/09/1916 | 19/10/1916 |
| War Diary | Merlimont Plage | 19/10/1916 | 31/01/1917 |
| War Diary | South of Merlimont | 30/01/1917 | 30/01/1917 |
| War Diary | Merlimont Plage | 01/02/1917 | 05/04/1917 |
| War Diary | St. Omer | 05/04/1917 | 08/04/1917 |
| War Diary | Ligny-St-Flochel | 08/04/1917 | 08/04/1917 |
| War Diary | Haute Avesnes | 08/04/1917 | 09/04/1917 |
| War Diary | Arras | 09/04/1917 | 10/04/1917 |
| War Diary | Arras-St. Pol. Road | 10/04/1917 | 10/04/1917 |
| War Diary | Tilloy | 11/04/1917 | 11/04/1917 |
| War Diary | Arras | 11/04/1917 | 11/04/1917 |
| War Diary | Tilloy | 11/04/1917 | 11/04/1917 |
| War Diary | Arras | 11/04/1917 | 11/04/1917 |
| War Diary | Arras. St. Pol Rd | 11/04/1917 | 12/04/1917 |
| War Diary | Fosseux | 12/04/1917 | 16/04/1917 |
| War Diary | Wavans | 16/04/1917 | 16/04/1917 |
| War Diary | Beauvoir Riviere | 16/04/1917 | 20/04/1917 |
| War Diary | Estrees-Les-Crecy | 20/04/1917 | 20/04/1917 |
| Miscellaneous | Reference Map No 51B Appendix | | |
| War Diary | Estrees-Les-Crecy | 01/05/1917 | 13/05/1917 |
| War Diary | Wavans | 13/05/1917 | 14/05/1917 |
| War Diary | La Vicogne | 14/05/1917 | 15/05/1917 |
| War Diary | Querrieu | 15/05/1917 | 17/05/1917 |
| War Diary | Lamotte-En-Santerre | 17/05/1917 | 19/05/1917 |
| War Diary | Flamicourt | 19/05/1917 | 30/06/1917 |
| War Diary | Dreslincourt | 01/06/1917 | 04/06/1917 |
| War Diary | Hamel | 01/06/1917 | 29/06/1917 |

② 

WO 95/1146

3 Cavalry Division
Divisional Troops.
7 Light Armoured Battery
July 1916 – June 1917.

3RD CAVALRY DIVISION. WO95/1146

# 7TH LIGHT ARMOURED BATTERY.

## M.M.G.S.

### JULY 1916 – ~~JULY~~ JUNE 1917.

No 80+

B.E.F.

3 CAV DIV TROOPS

Army Form C. 2118.

# WAR DIARY
## or
## INTELLIGENCE SUMMARY.
*(Erase heading not required.)*

**7TH LIGHT ARMOURED BATTERY**
**M. M. G. S.**
**JULY 1916**

Instructions regarding War Diaries and Intelligence Summaries are contained in F. S. Regs., Part II. and the Staff Manual respectively. Title pages will be prepared in manuscript.

Vol I

| Place | Date | Hour | Summary of Events and Information | Remarks and references to Appendices |
|---|---|---|---|---|
| CORBIE | 1.7.16 | | LIEUT. TOD moved out and reconnoitred to ALBERT and reconnoitred the general lie of the country with a view to the armoured cars being used in that vicinity. | |
| Do | 10.7.16 | | Reft CORBIE for HALLENCOURT alongwith 3RD CAVALRY DIVISION | |
| HALLENCOURT | 11.7.16 | 1 p.m. | Reft HALLENCOURT for DAOURS. | |
| DAOURS | 11.7.16 | 10 a.m. | All cars were out on range at DAOURS for firing practice. | |
| Do | 13.7.16 | 10 a.m. | All cars were out on range at DAOURS for firing practice. 7 Br. HOTCHKISS Q.F. Also fired. CAPTAIN HENSHALL and 2/LIEUT. E. A. SAMSON carried out reconnaissance in vicinity of MARICOURT, MONTAUBAN, HIGH WOOD, FRICOURT and CONTALMAISON. | |
| Do | 15.7.16 | | CAPTAIN HENSHALL, LIEUT. DTOD and 2/LIEUT. E. A. SAMSON carried out reconnaissance in the neighbourhood of CARNOY – MONTAUBAN. | |
| Do | 16.7.16 | | Battery attached to XIII CORPS. | |
| Do | 17.7.16 | 11.30 a.m. | Left DAOURS for BRONFAY FARM via ETINHEIM Attached to 3RD INFANTRY DIVISION and billeted in dug outs off BRAY – MARICOURT road 100 yards South of BRONFAY FARM. | |
| BRONFAY FARM | 25.7.16 | | Shells dropped on BRONFAY FARM. German Prisoners lodged there removed after | |

**WAR DIARY**
or
**INTELLIGENCE SUMMARY.**

7TH LIGHT ARMOURED BATTERY
M.M.G.S.
JULY, 1916. (CONTINUED)

Army Form C. 2118.

| Place | Date | Hour | Summary of Events and Information | Remarks and references to Appendices |
|---|---|---|---|---|
| BRONFAY FARM | 25.7.16 | — | several casualties. | |
| D° | 26.7.16 | 2.30pm | Battery prepared to move H.q. on Left. Bronfay Farm for Daours. Again attached to 3rd Cavalry Division. | |
| | | | In DAOURS until 31st July 1916. | |

Arthur Rankin CAPT.
COMDG. 7TH LIGHT ARMOURED BATTERY,
M.M.G.S.

**WAR DIARY**
or
**INTELLIGENCE SUMMARY.**
(Erase heading not required.)

Army Form C. 2118.

7TH LIGHT ARMOURED BATTERY
M.M.G.S.

AUGUST, 1916.

Instructions regarding War Diaries and Intelligence Summaries are contained in F. S. Regs., Part II. and the Staff Manual respectively. Title pages will be prepared in manuscript.

| Place | Date | Hour | Summary of Events and Information | Remarks and references to Appendices |
|---|---|---|---|---|
| DROURS | 1.8.16 | | Proceeded to GARENNES, PAS DE CALAIS. | |
| GARENNES | 4.8.16 | | Proceeded to COUPELLE NEUVE, PAR FRUGES, PAS DE CALAIS. Remained at COUPELLE NEUVE, till end of month. | |
| | | | Note. During month all Armoured Cars proceeded to CALAIS, PAS DE CALAIS, for fitment of some casings (armoured) to Machine Guns. | |
| | | | On 6th August, 1916, the Guns Maxim .303" held on charge of Battery were replaced by six Guns VICKERS .303" | |
| COUPELLE NEUVE | 10.8.16 | | CAPTAIN L.S. HENSHALL and 2/LIEUT. E.A. SAMSON, attended Tactical Exercise for Machine Gun Squadrons and Light Armoured Car Batteries. | |
| | 14.8.16 | | CAPTAIN L.S. HENSHALL attended Divisional Staff Exercise. (3rd Cav. Div.) | |
| | 21.8.16 | | CAPTAIN L.S. HENSHALL attended Divisional Staff Exercise. (3rd Cav. Div.) | |
| | 26.8.16 | | CAPTAIN L.S. HENSHALL attended Divisional Staff Exercise. (3rd Cav. Div.) | |

CAPT.
Comdg. 7th LIGHT ARMOURED BATTERY,
M.M.G.S.

Army Form C. 2118.

# WAR DIARY
## or
## INTELLIGENCE SUMMARY.
(Erase heading not required.)

7TH LIGHT ARMOURED BATTERY
M.M.G.S.
SEPTEMBER, 1916.

Vol 3

Instructions regarding War Diaries and Intelligence Summaries are contained in F.S. Regs., Part II. and the Staff Manual respectively. Title pages will be prepared in manuscript.

| Place | Date | Hour | Summary of Events and Information | Remarks and references to Appendices |
|---|---|---|---|---|
| COUPELLE NEUVE | 1.9.16 | — | | |
| Do. | 11.9.16 | 1.15pm | Proceeded to NEUILLY-LE-DIEU | |
| NEUILLY-LE-DIEU | 12.9.16 | 9am | Proceeded to BELLOY-SUR-SOMME | |
| BELLOY-SUR-SOMME | | | | |
| SOMME | 14.9.16 | 1P.M | Proceeded to VECQUEMONT, (SOMME) | |
| VECQUEMONT | 15.9.16 | 10.30am | Proceeded to LA NEUVILLE, (CORBIE SOMME) | |
| LA NEUVILLE | 19.9.16 | 6.45am | Returned to VECQUEMONT | |
| VECQUEMONT | 22.9.16 | 3.30pm | Proceeded to CROUY via AMIENS | |
| CROUY | 23.9.16 | 9.7am | Proceeded to VILLERS L'HOPITAL | |
| VILLERS L'HOPITAL | 24.9.16 | 11.15am | Proceeded to REGNAUVILLE | |
| REGNAUVILLE | 25.9.16 | 9pm | Proceeded to WAILLY-BEAUCAMP | |
| WAILLY-BEAUCAMP | | | Until 30.9.16. | |

[Signature] CAPT.
COMDG. 7TH LIGHT ARMOURED BATTERY,
M.M.G.S.

# WAR DIARY
## or
## INTELLIGENCE SUMMARY.
(Erase heading not required.)

Army Form C. 2118.

7TH LIGHT ARMOURED BATTERY
M.M.G.S.
OCTOBER, 1916.

Vol 4

| Place | Date | Hour | Summary of Events and Information | Remarks and references to Appendices |
|---|---|---|---|---|
| WAILLY-BEAUCAMP | 1.10.16 | | | |
| " | 19.10.16 | 9am | Proceeded to Mierlimont Plage. | |
| MIERLIMONT PLAGE | 19.10.16 | | | |
| " | 31.10.16 | | | |

Robt Sampson Lieut.
COMDG. 7TH LIGHT ARMOURED BATTERY.
M.M.G.S.

Army Form C. 2118.

# WAR DIARY
## or
## INTELLIGENCE SUMMARY
*(Erase heading not required.)*

**7th LIGHT ARMOURED BATTERY**
**M. M. G. S.**

Vol 5

Instructions regarding War Diaries and Intelligence Summaries are contained in F. S. Regs., Part II. and the Staff Manual respectively. Title pages will be prepared in manuscript.

| Place | Date | Hour | Summary of Events and Information | Remarks and references to Appendices |
|---|---|---|---|---|
| MERSIMONT PLAGE | 1-11-16 to 30-11-16 | | In Winter Quarters | |

[signature] CAPT.
COMDG. 7TH LIGHT ARMOURED BATTERY,
M.M.G.S.

Army Form C. 2118.

# WAR DIARY
## or
## ~~INTELLIGENCE SUMMARY~~

*(Erase heading not required.)*

7TH LIGHT ARMOURED BATTERY
M. M. G. S.

No. 1 6

Instructions regarding War Diaries and Intelligence Summaries are contained in F. S. Regs., Part II. and the Staff Manual respectively. Title pages will be prepared in manuscript.

| Place | Date | Hour | Summary of Events and Information | Remarks and references to Appendices |
|---|---|---|---|---|
| MERRIMONT PLAGE | 1-12-16 TO 31-12-16 | | IN WINTER QUARTERS. | |

[signature]
COMDg. 7TH LIGHT ARMOURED BATTERY,
CAPT.
M. M. G. S.

Army Form C. 2118.

# WAR DIARY
## or
## ~~INTELLIGENCE SUMMARY~~.
*(Erase heading not required.)*

7TH LIGHT ARMOURED BATTERY
M.M.G.S.

Vol 7

Instructions regarding War Diaries and Intelligence Summaries are contained in F. S. Regs., Part II. and the Staff Manual respectively. Title pages will be prepared in manuscript.

| Place | Date | Hour | Summary of Events and Information | Remarks and references to Appendices |
|---|---|---|---|---|
| MERRIMONT | 1-1-17 to 31-1-17 | | IN WINTER QUARTERS. | |
| SOUTH OF MERRIMONT | 30-1-17 | 2.30pm | INSPECTION OF BATTERY BY G.O.C. 3RD CAVALRY DIV. AND ITALIAN CAVALRY OFFICER. | |

[signature], CAPT.
COMDG. 7TH LIGHT ARMOURED BATTERY,
M.M.G.S.

Army Form C. 2118.

Vol 8

WAR DIARY
or
INTELLIGENCE SUMMARY.
(Erase heading not required.)

7TH LIGHT ARMOURED BATTERY
M. M. G. S.

Instructions regarding War Diaries and Intelligence Summaries are contained in F. S. Regs., Part II. and the Staff Manual respectively. Title pages will be prepared in manuscript.

| Place | Date | Hour | Summary of Events and Information | Remarks and references to Appendices |
|---|---|---|---|---|
| MERLIMONT PLAGE. | 1-2-17 to 28-2-17 | | IN WINTER QUARTERS. | |
| MERLIMONT PLAGE. | 2-2-17 | 11 A.M. | INSPECTION OF BATTERY BY AMERICAN MILITARY ATTACHÉ. | |
| MERLIMONT PLAGE. | 16-2-17 | 3 P.M. | INSPECTION OF BATTERY BY COL. McMULLEN G.H.Q. | |

[signature] CAPT.
COMDG. 7TH LIGHT ARMOURED BATTERY,
M. M. G. S.

Army Form C. 2118.

# WAR DIARY
## or
## INTELLIGENCE SUMMARY.
(Erase heading not required.)

7TH LIGHT ARMOURED BATTERY
M.M.G.S.

MARCH 1917

Vol 9

Instructions regarding War Diaries and Intelligence Summaries are contained in F.S. Regs., Part II. and the Staff Manual respectively. Title pages will be prepared in manuscript.

| Place | Date | Hour | Summary of Events and Information | Remarks and references to Appendices |
|---|---|---|---|---|
| MARJUMONT RIDGE | 1-3-17 to 31-3-17 | - | IN WINTER QUARTERS. | |

[signature] CAPT.
COMDG. 7TH LIGHT ARMOURED BATTERY.
M.M.G.S.

Army Form C. 2118.

# WAR DIARY
## or
## INTELLIGENCE SUMMARY.
*(Erase heading not required.)*

April — 7TH LIGHT ARMOURED BATTERY  
M. M. G. S.

Vol 10

| Place | Date | Hour | Summary of Events and Information | Remarks and references to Appendices |
|---|---|---|---|---|
| MERRIMONT PLAGE | 1-4-17 TO 4-4-14 | | } IN WINTER QUARTERS. | |
| MERRIMONT PLAGE | 5-4-14 | 1 A.M. | LEFT FOR ST. OMER VIA ETRABAS AND HESDIN. | |
| ST. OMER | 5-4-14 | 10.30 AM | ARRIVED AND PROCEEDED TO 3RD A.S.C. REPAIR SHOP. | |
| ST. OMER | 6-4-14 TO 7-4-14 | | ARMOURED CARS COVERED WITH URANITE. | |
| ST. OMER | 8-4-14 | 4.50 AM | LEFT FOR LIGNY-ST-FROCHEL VIA FRUGES AND ST. POL. | |
| LIGNY-ST-FROCHEL | -1- | 3 PM | ARRIVED | |
| LIGNY-ST-FROCHEL | -1- | 3.46 AM | PROCEEDED TO HAUTE-AVESNES | |
| HAUTE AVESNES | -1- | 6 PM | ARRIVED | |
| HAUTE AVESNES | 9-4-14 | 5.15 PM | ARMOURED CARS AND LIGHT TRANSPORT PROCEEDED TO ARRAS. HEAVY TRANSPORT LEFT AT HAUTE AVESNES | |
| ARRAS. | -1- | 8.30 PM | ARRIVED. CARS PARKED ON ARRAS-CAMBRAI ROAD. | |
| ARRAS | 10-4-14 | 1 A.M. | LEFT ARRAS. PARKED ON ARRAS - ST. POL ROAD | |
| ARRAS - ST. POL ROAD | 10-4-14 | 12 NOON | LEFT ARRAS-ST. POL ROAD FOR ARRAS. LIGHT TRANSPORT PARKED ON ARRAS-CAMBRAI ROAD. ARMOURED CARS PROCEEDED TO TILLOY. VIDE APPENDIX. | REFERENCE APPENDIX (I) |
| TILLOY | 11-4-14 | 7 A.M. | THREE ARMOURED CARS RETURNED TO ARRAS. REMAINING TWO STANDING BY AT TILLOY. | |

Army Form C. 2118.

# WAR DIARY
## or
## INTELLIGENCE SUMMARY.
*(Erase heading not required.)*

Instructions regarding War Diaries and Intelligence Summaries are contained in F. S. Regs., Part II. and the Staff Manual respectively. Title pages will be prepared in manuscript.

| Place | Date | Hour | Summary of Events and Information | Remarks and references to Appendices |
|---|---|---|---|---|
| ARRAS | 11.4.14 | 1.30pm | THE THIRD ARMOURED CARS RETURNED TO TINLOY | |
| TINLOY | -"- | 8.30pm | ARMOURED CARS LEFT TINLOY, WITH EXCEPTION OF RED CAR, FOR ARRAS. | |
| ARRAS | -"- | 6.30pm | ARMOURED CARS ARRIVED AND PROCEEDED TO ARRAS-ST.POL ROAD, WITH LIGHT TRANSPORTS | |
| ARRAS-ST.POL RD. | -"- | 6.0pm | ARRIVED AND PARKED | |
| ARRAS-ST.POL RD. | 12.4.14 | 10.30pm | PROCEEDED TO FOSSEUX | |
| FOSSEUX | 12.4.14 | 1 PM. | ARRIVED. CARS PARKED BY CHURCH. HEAVY TRANSPORT REJOINED BATTERY | |
| FOSSEUX | 13.4.14 TO 16.4.14 | | AT FOSSEUX. | |
| FOSSEUX | 16.4.14 | 1.30PM | PROCEEDED TO WAVANS | |
| WAVANS | -"- | 4.30PM | ARRIVED | |
| WAVANS | -"- | 4.0PM | PROCEEDED TO BEAUVOIR RIVIERE. | |
| BEAUVOIR RIVIERE | -"- | 4.30PM | ARRIVED. | |
| BEAUVOIR RIVIERE | 16.4.14 TO 20.4.14 | | AT BEAUVOIR RIVIERE. | |
| BEAUVOIR RIVIERE | 20.4.14 | 2.15PM | LEFT FOR ESTREES- LES- CRECY. | |
| ESTREES-LES-CRECY | 20.4.14 | 4.15PM | ARRIVED AND REMAINED TILL END OF MONTH. | |

*(signature)* CAPT.
COMDG. 7TH LIGHT ARMOURED BATTERY.
M. M. G. S.

I

## APPENDIX.

REFERENCE MAP No 51B 1/40,000

10-4-14.

On the morning of Tuesday April 10th 1914, the battery was ordered to report at SQUARE, 100 YDS N OF RAILWAY STATION ARRAS and await orders.

At 2pm orders were received to proceed on ARRAS-CAMBRAI road and on arrival at TILLOY to report again to advanced D.H.Q.

Owing to congestion of traffic and state of roads, it was impossible for the cars to keep their formation in column of route.

At TILLOY instructions were received to act in co-operation with 6th Brigade and for one section to proceed along and reconnoitre ARRAS-CAMBRAI road as far as possible to VIS-EN-ARTOIS, No 2 section to stand by at TILLOY.

Again owing to state of roads – shell holes – fallen trees – it was with the greatest difficulty that one car reached LA BERGERE.

Communication by means of the battery motor cycle despatch riders was impossible as they could not follow owing to mud.

II

The car which reached LA BERGERE fired at Germans crossing road 150 YDS E of GUÉMAPPE - MONCHY crossing and also traversed hedges on either side of road.

Dusk and heavy snow storm which filled observation slits made any further activity impossible for the time.

It was decided to report the situation to advanced 112th INFANTRY BRIGADE HEADQUARTERS and return to LA BERGERE.

Return was rendered impossible owing to complete darkness.

At 112th INFANTRY BRIGADE HEADQUARTERS Officer I/c remainder of No 1 Section was met and reported the position and state of his cars.

11-4-14

It having been decided at 4 A.M. that No 1 Section was not mechanically fit, without adjustments and repair, to proceed, this was reported, and orders were given for this Section to return to ARRAS for these repairs to be done as soon as possible and return, — leaving No 2 Section standing by at D.H.Q.

At 1.30 P.M. No 2 Section attempted to advance but again owing

III

the road conditions failed to reach its objective.

Road conditions were such, during the whole period of operations, that with the exception of the drivers, the personnel of the cars was constantly outside guiding and making up road surface.

Edward Samson, CAPT.
COMDG. 7TH LIGHT ARMOURED BATTERY,
M.M.G.S.

**WAR DIARY**
or
**INTELLIGENCE SUMMARY.**
(Erase heading not required.)

7TH LIGHT ARMOURED BATTERY Army Form C. 2118.
M. M. G. S.

MAY 1917.  Vol XI

| Place | Date | Hour | Summary of Events and Information | Remarks and references to Appendices |
|---|---|---|---|---|
| Estrees-Lès-Crecy | 1-5-17 to 12.5.17 | | In Rest Billets. | |
| — | 13.5.17 | 2.30 | Left Estrees-Lès-Crecy. | |
| Wavans | 13.5.17 | 4.15 | Arrived Wavans | |
| — | 14.5.17 | 2.0 | Left Wavans | |
| La Vicogne | 14.5.17 | 4.10 | Arrived La Vicogne | |
| — | 16.5.17 | 2.30 | Left La Vicogne | |
| Querrieu | 16.5.17 | 4.10 | Arrived Querrieu | |
| — | 17.5.17 | 3.0 | Left Querrieu | |
| Lamotte-en-Santerre | 17.5.17 | 4.0 | Arrived Lamotte-en-Santerre | |
| — | 18.5.17 | 10.30 | Armoured Cars left for St. Omer to undergo overhaul | |
| — | 19.5.17 | 10.30 | Left Lamotte-en-Santerre | |
| Flamicourt | 19.5.17 | 2.0 | Arrived Flamicourt. | |
| — | 22.5.17 | 10.30 | Sub-section Machine Guns left for Dreuincourt. Attached "N" Battery Anti-Aircraft. | |
| — | 23.5.17 | 4.30 | Sub-section Machine Guns left for Tincourt-Boucly. Attached "P" Battery Anti-Aircraft | |
| Flamicourt | 24.5.17 to 31.5.17 | | Headquarters of battery remained at Flamicourt. | |

[signature] Capt.
COMDG. 7TH LIGHT ARMOURED BATTERY
M.M.G.S.

Army Form C. 2118.

7TH LIGHT ARMOURED BATTERY

# WAR DIARY
## or
## INTELLIGENCE SUMMARY.
(Erase heading not required.)

JUNE

Vol 12

| Place | Date | Hour | Summary of Events and Information | Remarks and references to Appendices |
|---|---|---|---|---|
| FRANCICOURT | 1.6.17 TO 30.6.17 | | Head quarters of the Battery remained in Billets. | |
| DRESSINCOURT | 1.6.17 TO 4.6.17 | | Sub-Section Machine Guns Attached to 'N' Bty. Anti-Aircraft. | |
| HAMEL | 1.6.17 TO 29.6.17 | | Sub-Section Machine Guns Attached to 'P' Bty Anti-Aircraft. | |

[signature] Capt.
Comdg. 7th Light Armoured Battery
M.M.G.S.

www.ingramcontent.com/pod-product-compliance
Lightning Source LLC
Chambersburg PA
CBHW081252170426
43191CB00037B/2131